A Bad Lad

Written by Monica Hughes
Illustrated by Mike Byrne

T0373260

Fin is a bad lad.

Fin gets into the Cub hut.
Fin gets a cup and runs.

Fin gets into Rick's cabin.
Fin gets a laptop and runs.

"I can rob a bank."

Fin picks the lock, but
sets off the bell.

Stan gets his cuffs.
Stan runs to the bank.

Fin sobs and sobs.